DUDLEY SCHOOLS
LIBRARY SERVICE

KU-271-045

Schools Library and Information Services

S00000645145

Chemicals in Action

Elements & Compounds

Chris Oxlade

www.heinemann.co.uk/library
Visit our website to find out more information about **Heinemann Library** books.

To order:
☎ Phone 44 (0) 1865 888066
▤ Send a fax to 44 (0) 1865 314091
▢ Visit the Heinemann Bookshop at www.heinemann.co.uk/library to browse our
catalogue and order online.

First published in Great Britain by Heinemann Library, Halley Court, Jordan Hill, Oxford
OX2 8EJ, a division of Reed Educational and Professional Publishing Ltd. Heinemann is a
registered trademark of Reed Educational & Professional Publishing Limited.

OXFORD MELBOURNE AUCKLAND JOHANNESBURG BLANTYRE
GABORONE IBADAN PORTSMOUTH NH (USA) CHICAGO

© Reed Educational and Professional Publishing Ltd 2002
The moral right of the proprietor has been asserted.

All rights reserved. No part of this publication may be reproduced, stored in a retrieval system,
or transmitted in any form or by any means, electronic, mechanical, photocopying, recording,
or otherwise without either the prior written permission of the Publishers or a licence permitting
restricted copying in the United Kingdom issued by the Copyright Licensing Agency Ltd,
90 Tottenham Court Road, London W1P 0LP.

Designed by Tinstar Design (www.tinstar.co.uk)
Illustrations by Jeff Edwards.
Originated by Ambassador Litho Ltd.
Printed by Wing King Tong in Hong Kong.

ISBN 0 431 136025
06 05 04 03 02
10 9 8 7 6 5 4 3 2 1

DUDLEY PUBLIC LIBRARIES

L 46162

645/45   SCH

J546

British Library Cataloguing in Publication Data
Oxlade, Chris
Elements and compounds. – (Chemicals in action)
1. Chemical elements – Juvenile literature
I. Title
546

Acknowledgements
The Publishers would like to thank the following for permission to reproduce photographs:

Andrew Lambert pp9, 11, 29, Anthony Blake (Sue Atkinson) p34, Corbis p26, Culture Archive
p33, Photodisc p19, Popperfoto p20, Rex (Henry T Kaiser) p23 (top), Robert Harding p35,
Science Photo Library pp4, 5, 6, 7, 21, 23 (bottom), 24, 25, 30, 32, 36, 38, Telegraph Colour
Library pp12, 13, 18, 22, Trevor Clifford pp15, 17, 27, 29, 31, 37, 39.

Cover photograph reproduced with permission of Geoscience.

The Publishers would like to thank Dr Nigel Saunders for his assistance in the preparation of
this book.

Every effort has been made to contact copyright holders of any material reproduced in this
book. Any omissions will be rectified in subsequent printings if notice is given to the Publisher.

Contents

Words appearing in the text in bold, **like this**, are explained in the glossary.

Chemicals in action

What's the link between the Sun, an X-ray of a stomach, beautifully coloured fireworks, and even inks in your pens? The answer is **elements** and **compounds**. They all contain elements and compounds. In fact, all substances are made of elements and compounds, or a mixture of the two. Our knowledge of the different elements and compounds is used in making chemicals, in medical research, and in engineering.

The study of elements and compounds is part of the science of chemistry. Many people think of chemistry as something that scientists study by doing experiments in labs full of test tubes and flasks of bubbling liquids. This part of chemistry is very important. It is how scientists find out what substances are made of and how they make new materials, but this is only a tiny part of chemistry. Most chemistry happens away from laboratories, in factories and chemical plants. It is used to manufacture an enormous range of items, such as synthetic fibres for fabrics, drugs to treat diseases, explosives for fireworks, solvents for paints, and fertilizers for growing crops.

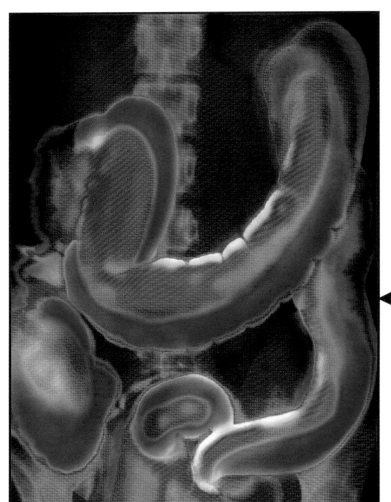

The shape of this patient's stomach and intestines shows up on an X-ray because he or she has just eaten a meal containing the element barium.

About the experiments

There are several experiments in the book for you to try. Doing these experiments will help you to understand some of the chemistry in the book. An experiment is designed to help solve a scientific problem. Scientists use a logical approach to experiments so that they can conclude things from the results of the experiments. A scientist first writes down a hypothesis, which he or she thinks might be the answer to the problem, then designs an experiment to test the hypothesis. He or she then writes down the results of the experiment and concludes whether the results show that hypothesis is true or not. We only know what we do about chemistry because scientists have carefully carried out thousands of experiments over hundreds of years.

Experiments have allowed scientists to discover all the hundred or more elements we know about, how they combine to make compounds, and even to make new elements.

Doing the experiments

All the experiments in this book have been designed for you to do at home with everyday substances and equipment. They can also be done in the school laboratory. Always follow the safety advice given with each experiment, and ask an adult to help you when the instructions tell you to.

A rocket is crammed full of chemicals that combine together to release the energy that lifts it off the ground.

Elements, compounds and mixtures

Every substance on the Earth (and the Earth itself!) is made up of tiny **particles** called **atoms**. Scientists have found 92 different types of atom that occur naturally on Earth and have made a few more, under special conditions in the laboratory. Atoms make up substances called **elements**, **compounds** and **mixtures**.

An element is a substance made up of just one type of atom. For example, oxygen is an element because it contains only oxygen atoms. An element is the most simple type of substance there is.

The scene near the top of a volcano. The yellow bits are crystals of the element sulfur.

A compound is a substance made up of different elements joined together. For example, water is a compound made up of the elements oxygen and hydrogen. The atoms of these two elements are joined together to form water and these joins are called chemical **bonds**. Compounds can be separated into simpler substances, such as elements or simpler compounds, by breaking these chemical bonds.

Building with elements

You could think of elements as coloured building blocks. Each element would be represented by a block with a **unique** colour, different to the blocks representing the other elements. A compound would contain blocks of different colours joined together.

By combining any two colours, or three colours, or more, you could build millions of different compounds. So you can see that although there are only a hundred or so different elements on Earth, they can combine to make millions of different compounds. Each different compound also contains a particular proportion of elements. For example, water always contains two lots of hydrogen and one lot of oxygen.

Mixtures

In science, a mixture is a substance that contains different elements and compounds that are *not* joined together by chemical bonds. A mixture of two different elements is not a compound because the elements are not joined by bonds. The air that you breathe is an example of a mixture. It contains some elements, such as oxygen and nitrogen, and some compounds, such as carbon dioxide. A mixture can always be separated into the individual substances it contains.

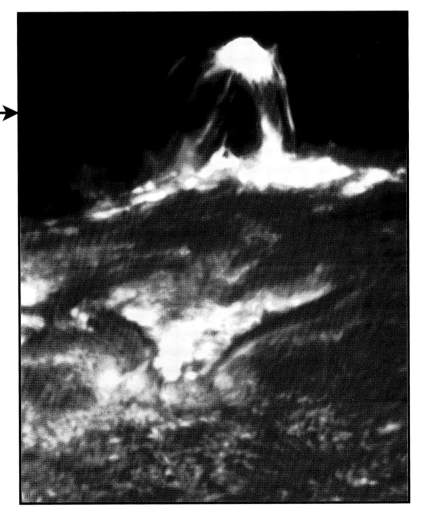

All the stars (including our Sun), the planets and moons in the universe are made of the same elements and compounds as the ones found on Earth. This solar flare erupting from the Sun's surface contains elements that can be found on Earth.

Atoms and molecules

All substances, whether they are **elements**, **compounds** or **mixtures**, are made up of tiny **particles**. These particles are either individual **atoms**, or groups of atoms called **molecules**. An atom is the smallest particle of an element that can exist. Imagine breaking up a piece of iron, into smaller and smaller pieces. Eventually you would end up with individual atoms. These would still be the element iron – but if you broke the atom into pieces (which would be extremely difficult) it would stop being iron.

Atoms are incredibly small. Even big ones are less than a millionth of a millimetre across. They are so small that the full stop at the end of this sentence contains millions and millions of atoms of the elements that make up the ink.

Molecules

A molecule is a particle made up of two or more atoms joined to each other with chemical **bonds**. The simplest molecules are made up of two atoms of the same element. For example, the gas oxygen is made up of oxygen molecules and each of these molecules is made up of two oxygen atoms joined together. The **symbol** for the element oxygen is O, but the **formula** for oxygen gas is O_2, to show that it is made up of molecules with two oxygen atoms. The molecules of some substances, such as plastics, contain thousands of atoms.

Inside an atom

Atoms are made up of even tinier particles called **protons**, **neutrons** and **electrons**. They are called sub-atomic particles. At the centre of every atom is a nucleus – made up of protons and neutrons joined together in a clump. Electrons whiz around the nucleus.

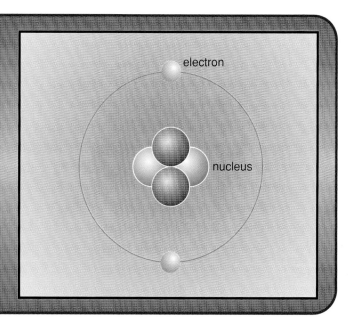

electron

nucleus

Elements, a compound and a mixture

1 Iron (a grey **metal**) and sulfur (a solid, yellow **non-metal**) are both elements. This is a mixture of iron filings and sulfur powder. The iron and sulfur are not chemically combined. They can be separated with a magnet, which picks up the iron.

2 If a mixture of iron filings and sulfur powder is heated, a chemical reaction starts. It continues until the iron and sulfur are used up. A grey solid is left. This is iron sulfide, which is a compound. It is made up of the same elements as the original mixture, but now the elements are joined by chemical bonds. The iron cannot be separated using a magnet.

Classifying elements

Every **element** has a name and a **symbol**. The symbol is an abbreviation (a shortened version) of the element's name. It is used to represent the element in chemical **formulae** and equations. For example, the chemical symbol for the element carbon is C. The symbols of elements do not always seem to match the elements' names though. This is because the symbols come from different languages. For example, the symbol for iron is Fe, which comes from *ferro*, the Greek word for iron.

The periodic table

The periodic table is a list of all the known elements. The elements are arranged so that elements with similar **properties** to each other are close together. For example, fluorine (F) and chlorine (Cl) are gases that react very easily with other elements and so are close together in the table. The periodic table gets its name from the fact that the properties the elements have repeat themselves every few elements, or periodically. A chemist can tell what the properties of an element are likely to be by looking at its position in the table.

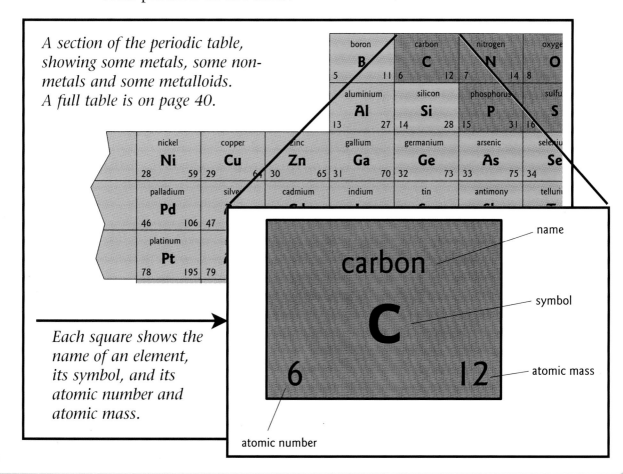

A section of the periodic table, showing some metals, some non-metals and some metalloids. A full table is on page 40.

Each square shows the name of an element, its symbol, and its atomic number and atomic mass.

name

symbol

atomic mass

atomic number

Chlorine (rear), bromine, and iodine (front) have similar chemical properties. They are all members of group 7 of the periodic table.

Groups and periods

The vertical columns of elements are called groups. The horizontal rows of elements are called periods. The table also shows which elements are **metals**, which are **non-metals** and which are **metalloids** (you can find out more about these on page 13). Some groups have special names:

Group 1: The alkali metals
Group 2: The alkaline earth metals
Group 7: The halogens
Group 0: The noble gases

Inventing a table

In 1829, a German chemist called Johann Wolfgang Döbereiner (1780–1849) noticed that some elements could be put into groups of three elements, each with similar properties. He called these groups, 'triads'. In 1864, an English chemist called John Newlands (1837–1898) arranged the elements known at the time into order of the masses of their atoms. He found that each element had properties like the element eight places in front of it, so he called this his 'Law of Octaves' (because it was like eight musical notes in an octave). In 1868, the Russian chemist Dimitri Mendeleyev (1834–1907) spotted more patterns in the behaviour of the elements that had been discovered at the time. He drew up the first periodic table that showed elements with similar properties in columns.

Metals and non-metals

The **elements** in the periodic table are divided into two main groups. They are the **metals** and the **non-metals**. About three-quarters of the elements are metals and these appear on the left-hand side of the periodic table. The non-metals appear on the right-hand side.

The properties of metals

All metals look shiny. Sometimes the shine on the surface of a piece of metal gradually disappears as the metal reacts with oxygen in the air. The shine comes back if the metal is polished, and if it is cut open the metal that is revealed is also shiny. Most metals are very hard, but a few are so soft that you can cut into them with a knife. Metals are also malleable, which means they can be bent or beaten into different shapes without breaking.

All metals are solids at room temperature except mercury, which is a liquid. This is because metals have high **melting points**. For example, the melting point of iron is 1535°C. Metals also have high **boiling points**. Iron boils at 2861°C. All metals let heat and electricity pass through them easily and are therefore described as being good **conductors** of heat and electricity. Only a very few metals, such as iron, are magnetic, which means they are attracted by magnets.

Copper is an extremely good conductor of electricity. These copper rods will be made into copper wire for cables.

The properties of non-metals

All metals have similar **properties** to each other. Non-metals however, have a wide range of different properties. For example, they come in several different colours. At room temperature most non-metals are gases, some are solids and one (bromine) is a liquid. This is because non-metals have a wide range of melting and boiling points. For example, sulfur is a solid at room temperature because its melting point is 113°C, and nitrogen is a gas at room temperature because its boiling point is -196°C. Non-metals do not conduct electricity or heat well. Carbon is an exception because it conducts electricity just as well as metal. No non-metals are magnetic.

Metalloids

A few elements, such as silicon, have some of the properties of metals and some of the properties of non-metals. They are not really metals and not really non-metals. They are called **metalloids** or semi-metals.

Their most important use is in making materials called semiconductors. A semiconductor is a material that can conduct some electricity compared to an **insulator**, but not as well as metals, which are good conductors. Semiconductors are used in electronic components and microchips.

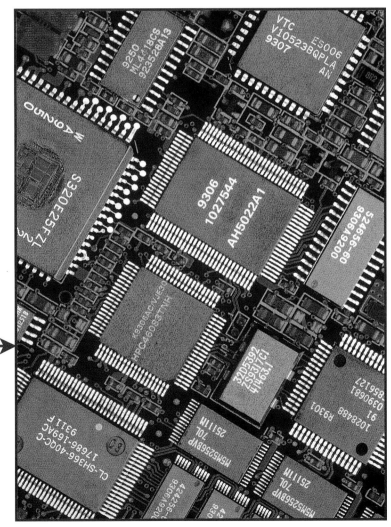

Microchips on a complex circuit board. The semiconductor chips themselves are encased in protective plastic.

Metals in reactions

Some **metals** react very well with common chemicals such as **acids**, the air and water. Other metals don't react with chemicals at all. The **reactivity series** (see below) is a list of common metals in order of how well they react, or how reactive they are.

Metals at the top of the series, such as potassium and sodium, are extremely reactive. These metals are found in group 1 of the periodic table. They react quickly with the air to make metal **oxides** and have to be stored in oil to keep the air away from them. They fizz strongly when they are put in water and react violently when they are placed in acid. These reactions make hydrogen gas and lots of heat. The heat ignites the hydrogen, making it explode.

Metals at the bottom of the reactivity series, such as gold and silver, are not reactive at all. They don't even react with strong acids such as hydrochloric acid. These unreactive metals all come from the large block in the centre of the periodic table called the transition metals.

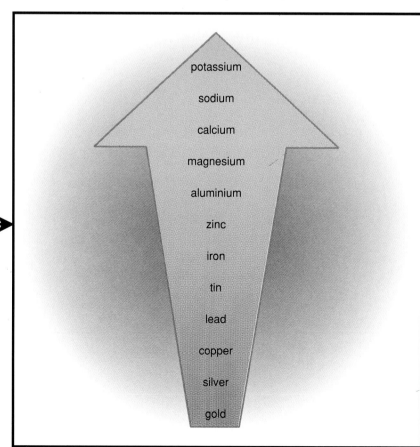

The reactivity series of common metals. It shows, for example, that aluminium is more reactive than zinc, but less reactive than magnesium.

potassium
sodium
calcium
magnesium
aluminium
zinc
iron
tin
lead
copper
silver
gold

Experiment: Reactive metals

PROBLEM: Which common metals are most reactive?

HYPOTHESIS: To find which metals are most reactive, we can put pieces of the metals in a weak acid and watch what happens. The one that fizzes most quickly will be the most reactive.

EQUIPMENT
nail or screw made of iron or steel
galvanized (zinc-coated) nail or screw
nail or screw made of copper or brass
white vinegar (coloured vinegar will work)
three small jars
one bowl

Experiment steps

1 Put a nail or screw into each of the three small jars. Pour just enough vinegar into the jars to cover the nails or screws. Watch what happens over a few minutes. While you are waiting, ask an adult to heat a kettle of water (it does not need to boil).

2 Make sure a window is open because the next bit gets really smelly! Ask the adult to pour some hot water into the bowl. Carefully put your jars into the water so that the hot water will heat up the vinegar in the jars. Again, watch what happens over a few minutes. Take care not to breathe deeply near the warm vinegar.

3 Make a note of your results. If bubbles are coming off the surface of the metal, there is a reaction happening. You can make sure by gently swirling the vinegar to remove any bubbles. Then watch to see if they start coming off on their own again. Write down whether the reaction is fast, steady or slow, or whether there is no reaction at all.

4 Write down the three metals in order of their speeds of reaction, starting your list with the most reactive and working down to the least reactive. This is your reactivity series.

CONCLUSION: Zinc fizzes quite quickly so is the most reactive of the three metals. Iron fizzes a little bit. Copper does not fizz at all, so is the least reactive.

Elements on the Earth

There are 92 **elements** that occur naturally on the Earth. They are found in the rocks that make up the Earth's crust, in fresh and sea water, in the air that makes up the Earth's atmosphere and in animals and plants.

There are different amounts of each element on Earth. Some elements, such as oxygen and carbon, are found in large amounts and are easy to find. These are 'abundant' elements but many elements are only found in very tiny amounts. Some elements occur naturally, uncombined with other elements – normally as part of a **mixture** – for example gold, which is found in the ground, and oxygen, which is part of the air. However, most elements are found locked up in **compounds**.

Extracting elements

We use nearly all of the elements for one job or another in industry, medicine, agriculture and science. Before we can use them, we have to **extract** them from where they are found. This involves collecting the mixtures or compounds the elements are in, and then breaking them up to get the elements out. Many different chemical processes and physical processes are used to do this.

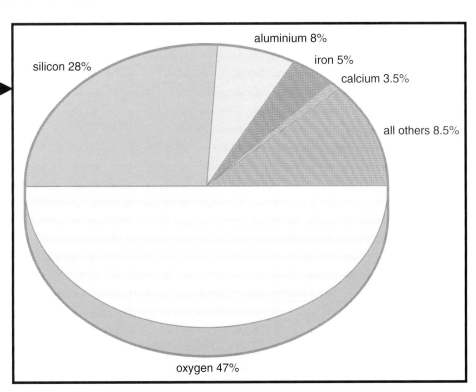

A pie chart of the most common elements in the Earth's crust. The element oxygen is the most common element found in the Earth's crust. All living things need this vital element to survive.

aluminium 8%

iron 5%

calcium 3.5%

silicon 28%

all others 8.5%

oxygen 47%

Experiment: Chlorine from salt water

PROBLEM: Where can we get chlorine from?

HYPOTHESIS: Chlorine is one of the elements in common salt, and sea water contains lots of dissolved common salt. So it may be possible to get chlorine by **electrolysis** of salt water.

Experiment steps

1 Pour water into the jar until it is 2cm below the rim. Stir in, and dissolve, one or two teaspoons of salt.

2 Wrap some aluminium foil around one of the jaws of the clothes peg. Slip the clothes peg over the rim of the jar so that the jaw with the foil is on the inside. Use the peg to clamp two propelling pencil leads to the inside of the jar (the peg should be above the salt **solution** and the leads should be in it).
Alternatively, sharpen a pencil at both ends and clamp this with the clothes peg (make sure that the top end of the pencil lead is in contact with the aluminium foil).
Cut a strip of aluminium foil about 20cm long and 2cm wide, wrap one end of this around the foil on the jaw but leave about 15cm free at the other end.

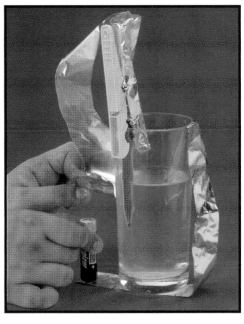

EQUIPMENT
pencil or propelling pencil leads
clothes peg
aluminium foil
battery
table salt
glass jar

3 Cut a strip of aluminium foil about 30cm long and 2cm wide. Push one end of the foil into the salt solution at the opposite end to the clothes peg, bend it over the rim of the jar, and pass it underneath.

4 Connect the + terminal of the battery to the aluminium foil running from the clothes peg, and connect the − terminal of the battery to the other piece of aluminium foil. Watch what happens.

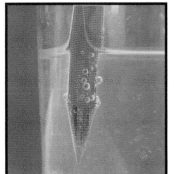

5 Tiny bubbles of gas form at each **electrode**. Smell (but not too closely) the gas coming from the pencil lead.

CONCLUSION: The gas that forms on the pencil lead is chlorine gas. It is formed by electrolysis of the salt (sodium chloride) solution.

Common metals

Metals are **extracted** from rocks in the Earth's crust. The rocks contain minerals called **ores**. An ore is a **compound** made up of a metal combined with other **elements**. The metals that we use most are the ones that have plenty of ores and are easiest to extract from their ores.

Metals are often mixed with each other or with **non-metals** to make materials called **alloys**. Alloys have more useful **properties** than the metals they are made from.

Iron

Iron is the most widely used metal of all. It is hard and grey, and the most common magnetic metal. Some iron is made into iron

objects such as gates and railings but most iron is made into steel. Steel is an alloy. It contains about 99 per cent iron and about 1 per cent carbon. Steel is made into cars, ships, buildings and hundreds of other objects. Iron's biggest problem is that it rusts quickly in damp air. Rusting is a reaction of the iron with oxygen and water. It eats away iron or steel, making it weak.

All modern high-rise buildings have a super-strong skeleton made of steel or concrete reinforced with steel.

Copper

Copper is a soft, brown metal that is easy to shape and cut. Copper is a very good **conductor** of electricity, so it is used to make wires and cables. It is also made into pipes for water supply and heating systems. Copper is mixed with zinc to make an alloy called brass. Brass does not lose its shine and is harder than copper or zinc.

Aluminium

Aluminium is a silver-coloured metal that has a low **density**. Most aluminium is made into drinks cans, pans and kitchen foil. The aluminium on the surface of an aluminium object slowly reacts with the air to form aluminium **oxide**. This forms a layer that protects the aluminium underneath.

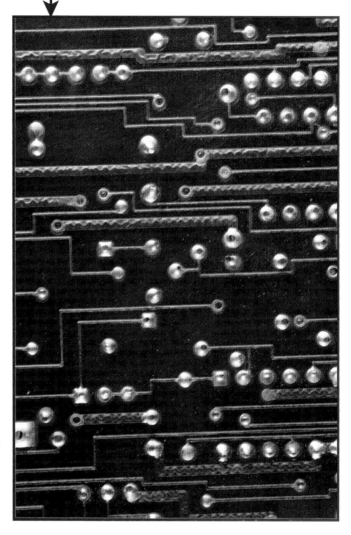

Gold conducts electricity extremely well and is often used in electronic circuits.

Discovering metals

The metals we know about today were discovered gradually over thousands of years. Most were discovered in the last two hundred years. Gold and silver were discovered more than five thousand years ago. This is because they are at the bottom of the **reactivity series** – they don't react with other elements to form compounds and so are easy to find as elements. Copper was discovered next. Copper is only slightly reactive and is released from its ore when the ore is heated. It was probably discovered by accident when a piece of ore was heated in a fire.

Common non-metals

Non-metal elements come from the air in the atmosphere, from sea water and from **ores** in rocks, like **metals** do. Many of the non-metals that are gases at room temperature, such as nitrogen and oxygen, can be found in the air. They are **extracted** by **fractional distillation** of the air.

Hydrogen

Hydrogen is the simplest of all the elements. It is also the most common element in the Universe. Each hydrogen **atom** is made up of one **proton** and one **electron**. At room temperature, hydrogen is a colourless, odourless gas that is very explosive. Hydrogen is used to make many different chemicals, including fertilizers. It is extracted from **natural gas**.

Giant airships of the 1930s were filled with explosive hydrogen gas. This airship – Hindenburg *burst into flames before landing, and this was not the only airship disaster to occur.*

Carbon

Carbon is an unusual and important element. It is found in two very different forms, diamond and graphite. Graphite is the substance that pencil leads are made from and is the only non-metal substance that conducts electricity. Diamond is used in jewellery and in the blades of cutting tools because it is extremely hard. Both diamond and graphite have **melting points** higher than most metals. The differences between diamond and graphite are caused by the carbon atoms being joined together in different ways. Carbon is the most important element for life and most of the compounds that make up animals and plants contain carbon. These are called **organic** compounds. You can find out more about them on page 32.

Nitrogen

Nitrogen is a colourless, odourless gas that makes up 78 per cent of the air in the atmosphere. Nitrogen is vital for plants because it is needed to build the compounds that make up plant **cells**. In industry, nitrogen is made by fractional distillation of air. It is used to make a compound called ammonia as well as nitric **acid**. These can be used to make fertilizers and explosives.

The drilling tip of a dentist's drill is coated with particles of diamond, a form of carbon.

Phosphorus

The element phosphorus is a solid that occurs in two common forms – white and red. White phosphorus is waxy, poisonous and very reactive. It has to be stored under water because it catches fire in the air. Red phosphorus is used to make matches and distress flares.

Fractional distillation

Fractional distillation is a process used to separate a **mixture** of liquids. It is the process used to extract gases from air, which itself is a mixture of gases. First, the air is cooled until it **condenses** to become a liquid. Then it is warmed up again gradually. Each gas in the mixture has a different **boiling point**. As the temperature of the liquid reaches the boiling point of one of the gases, that gas boils and is collected. Then the temperature is raised again and the next gas boils to be collected.

More non-metals

On these pages you can find out about more **non-metal elements**. They include the elements in group 7 of the periodic table, called the halogens, and group 0 of the periodic table, called the noble gases.

Oxygen

Oxygen is a colourless, odourless gas that makes up 21 per cent of the air. Oxygen is the part of the air that we use when we breathe, so is vital for life. Many substances react with oxygen when they are left open to the air. For example, burning is a reaction between a substance and oxygen in the air, which normally only happens if the substance is heated up. Oxygen is **extracted** from the air by **fractional distillation**. It is also the most common element in the rocks of the Earth's crust.

A major use of noble gases is in the bulbs of illuminated signs.

Normal oxygen **molecules** contain two oxygen **atoms**, but high in the atmosphere, oxygen is found as a gas called ozone – which has molecules made up of three oxygen atoms.

Sulfur

Sulfur is a yellow solid. It is found as an element in rocks, especially in areas of the world where there are volcanoes. You often see it on the surface around hot springs. Sulfur is used in the manufacture of sulfuric **acid**. It is also added to rubber in vehicle tyres to make the rubber more long-lasting.

The noble gases

The elements in group 0 of the periodic table are non-metal gases called the noble gases. They are all completely unreactive, so do not react with other elements to make **compounds**. Most noble gases are found in tiny amounts in the air, and are extracted by fractional distillation. Helium is extracted from **natural gas** by fractional distillation.

The halogens

The elements in group 7 of the periodic table are called the halogens and they include fluorine, chlorine, bromine and iodine. Fluorine is made into compounds used for non-stick coatings. Chlorine is used as a disinfectant because it kills **micro-organisms**. For example, small amounts of chlorine are dissolved in swimming pool water to kill bacteria that might spread disease from one swimmer to another. Fluorine and chlorine are very reactive. They are also poisonous in high concentrations when they are elements, but not when they are in compounds. Bromine is a brown liquid that gives off poisonous bromine gas. Iodine is a dark purple solid. It is important in our diets and is also used as an antiseptic.

Many makes of light bulb, including those used in car head-lights, are filled with halogen gases.

Joseph Priestley (1733–1804)

Joseph Priestley was a church minister, English teacher and chemist. He studied how gases were formed during **chemical reactions**. He discovered nitrogen in 1772 and oxygen in 1774. He found oxygen by heating mercury oxide, which divided into mercury and oxygen.

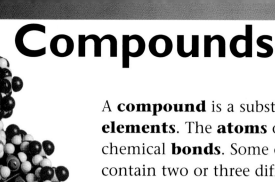

Compounds

A **compound** is a substance that is made up of different **elements**. The **atoms** of the elements are joined together by chemical **bonds**. Some compounds are very simple and might contain two or three different elements joined together in a simple way. For example, sodium chloride (common salt) is made up of just sodium and chlorine. A piece of salt contains one chlorine atom for every sodium atom. Its **formula** is NaCl. Other compounds are very complicated. They might contain several different elements joined together in different amounts. For example, the compound glucose, which is a type of sugar, is made up of carbon, hydrogen and oxygen. It contains one oxygen atom and two hydrogen atoms for every carbon atom. Its formula is $C_6H_{12}O_6$.

Making compounds

Compounds are made when different elements join together in **chemical reactions**. For example, when the element carbon burns, it combines with the element oxygen, from the air, to make the compound carbon dioxide.

carbon	+	oxygen	$\longrightarrow$	carbon dioxide
C	+	O_2	$\longrightarrow$	CO_2

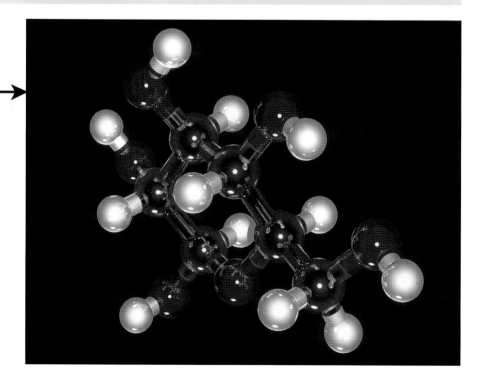

A model of a molecule of glucose ($C_6H_{12}O_6$).

Molecules and giant structures

Some compounds are made up of **molecules**. Remember that a molecule is a **particle** made up of atoms joined to each other. Each molecule of a compound contains one or more atoms of each element in the compound. Each molecule is the same as all the other molecules. For example, carbon dioxide is made up of molecules; every molecule of carbon dioxide is made of one carbon atom joined to two oxygen atoms.

Some compounds are not made up of molecules. Instead, each atom joins to all the atoms around it. The atoms build together to make a structure called a **lattice**. Often the atoms in a lattice turn into particles called **ions**. They do this by losing or gaining **electrons**. For example, sodium chloride is made of sodium ions and chlorine ions arranged in a lattice. Each sodium atom loses an electron and each chlorine atom gains one.

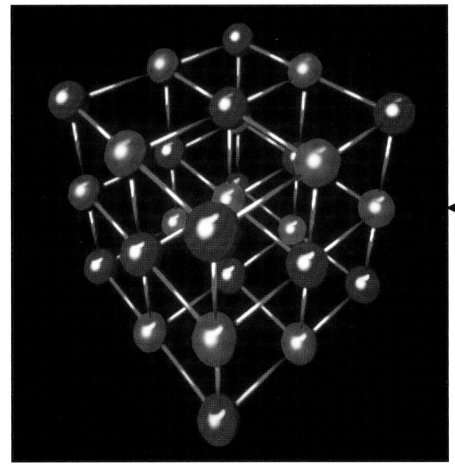

This computer graphic shows a model of part of a giant ionic lattice of sodium chloride. Sodium ions (in red) and chloride ions (in green) repeat themselves to create this lattice of sodium chloride.

Families of compounds

Simple **compounds** come in two main groups. One group is made up of compounds that contain a **metal element** combined with one or more **non-metal** elements. Examples of these compounds are iron sulfide (made up of the metal iron and the non-metal sulfur) and copper sulfate (made up of the metal copper and the non-metals sulfur and oxygen). The other group is made up of compounds that contain two or more non-metal elements combined together. Examples of these compounds are carbon dioxide (made up of the non-metals carbon and oxygen) and hydrogen chloride (made up of the non-metals hydrogen and chlorine). There are no compounds made up of metals combined with metals.

More families

Compounds are also put into groups or families because of the elements they contain. An **oxide** is a compound that contains a metal or a non-metal combined with oxygen. Aluminium oxide and carbon dioxide are examples of oxides. A carbonate is a compound that contains a metal combined with carbon and oxygen. Magnesium carbonate is an example of a carbonate. Sulfates and nitrates are similar to carbonates, but they contain sulfur or nitrogen instead of carbon.

A salt is a compound made when an **acid** reacts with a **base**. A base is often a metal oxide, and when a base dissolves in water it makes an **alkali**. A salt always contains a metal and a non-metal. Copper sulfate and sodium chloride are examples of salts.

These limestone cliffs are made up of calcium, carbon and oxygen in the form of calcium carbonate.

Experiment: Making a metal oxide

PROBLEM: How can we make a metal oxide?

HYPOTHESIS: Oxides are formed in a reaction between a substance and oxygen in the air. Heating a metal in the air should make an oxide.

Experiment steps

1 Tear a piece of aluminium kitchen foil about 30cm long and 1 to 2cm wide. Hold one end in a pair of tongs or wooden peg.

> **EQUIPMENT**
> aluminium kitchen foil
> kitchen tongs
> old saucer

2 An adult must do this step with you. Heat the last 1cm of the foil in the flame of a gas cooker hob for a few seconds and then remove it. Watch what happens.

3 Allow the aluminium to cool for about half a minute. Crumble the burned aluminium onto an old saucer. Can you see a grey powder?

CONCLUSION: The metal burns in the flame. The outer layer of the aluminium has combined with oxygen to make the compound aluminium oxide.

Compound names and formulae

You know that each **element** has a name and a **symbol** that is used to represent the element in chemical equations. **Compounds** also have names and **formulae**. The name of a compound contains the names of the elements that are in it. For example, iron **oxide** is a compound that contains the elements iron and oxygen, and sodium chloride is a compound that contains sodium and chlorine. Unfortunately, the compound names are not always easy to understand. Some compounds have common names, such as 'water', that do not tell you what elements the compounds contain.

Some compound names also tell you how many **atoms** of each element are in the compounds. For example, the 'mono' part of the name carbon monoxide tells you that the compound contains one oxygen atom for every carbon atom. Carbon and oxygen also form the compound carbon dioxide. The 'di' shows that carbon dioxide contains two oxygen atoms for every carbon atom.

Name endings

Compound names always end with letters such as 'ide' and 'ate'. The letters 'ide' mean that the compound contains two elements only. For example, copper oxide contains copper and oxygen only. The letters 'ate' mean that the compound contains oxygen as well. For example, calcium phosphate contains calcium, phosphorous and oxygen.

Compound formulae

Every compound has a formula made up of symbols (for elements) and numbers. The formula tells you what elements are in the compound and how many atoms of each element combine to make up the compound. Here are some examples of compound names, their formulae and the number of atoms of each element that combine to make up the compound:

Compound name	Formulae	Number of atoms of each element
carbon monoxide	CO	1 x C; 1 x O
carbon dioxide	CO_2	1 x C; 2 x O
calcium carbonate	$CaCO_3$	1 x Ca; 1 x C; 3 x O
calcium hydroxide	$Ca(OH)_2$	1 x Ca; 2 x O; 2 x H

In chemical equations you often see a number before the formula of a compound. This means that two lots of each atom in the compound take part in the equation. For example, H_2O is the formula for water and $2H_2O$ means two **molecules** of water, each containing two hydrogen atoms and one oxygen atom.

A model of a molecule of the compound carbon dioxide (CO_2) – it contains one atom of carbon and two atoms of oxygen.

A model of a molecule of the compound ammonia (NH_3) – it contains one atom of nitrogen and three atoms of hydrogen.

A model of a molecule of the compound ethane (C_2H_6) – it contains two atoms of carbon and six atoms of hydrogen.

A model of a molecule of the compound sulfuric acid (H_2SO_4) – it contains two atoms of hydrogen, one atom of sulfur and four atoms of oxygen.

Physical properties

The physical **properties** of an **element** or **compound** include its colour, texture, **density** and its **melting** and **boiling points**. Different elements have different physical properties to one another, and so do different compounds. Compounds also have very different properties to the elements they are made from. Some physical properties depend on how strongly the **particles** that make up the element or compound are joined together.

Melting and boiling points

Melting is turning from solid to liquid. It happens when a solid is hot enough for the **bonds** between the particles in the solid to begin to break, allowing the particles to move about. Boiling is turning from liquid to gas. It happens when a liquid is hot enough for the bonds between the particles in the liquid to break completely, allowing the particles to escape and form a gas.

Metallic elements have strong bonds between their **atoms**, and compounds made up of **ions** have strong bonds between their ions. They have high melting points and boiling points because the temperature must be very high before the bonds between the atoms or ions will break. This is why most metals, and **ionic compounds** such as sodium chloride, are solids at room temperature.

This is not ice, but solid carbon dioxide. Carbon dioxide has very low melting and boiling points, so it turns straight from a solid to a gas at room temperature.

Elements and compounds that are made up of simple **molecules** are different. There are strong bonds between the atoms that make up the molecules, but weak bonds between one molecule and the next. These elements and compounds have low melting and boiling points. This is why most compounds made of simple molecules are liquids or gases at room temperature.

Elements from compounds

1 The red solid in this test tube is mercury **oxide**. It is a compound of mercury and oxygen.

When the solid is heated it gradually begins to change. Shiny, liquid mercury begins to appear.

2 Eventually all of the solid is gone and only mercury is left. The oxygen, which is a gas, has escaped into the air. You can see that the properties of the elements in a compound are very different to the properties of the compound they make.

This type of reaction is called a **decomposition** reaction.

mercury oxide	$\longrightarrow$	mercury + oxygen
2HgO	$\longrightarrow$	2Hg + O$_2$

Organic compounds

Your body tissues, such as your skin and muscles, contain a huge collection of complicated **compounds** – and so do the tissues of all animals and plants. These compounds are called **organic** compounds. Organic compounds are also found in fossil fuels, such as oil and gas, because these fuels were formed from the remains of animals and plants. Organic chemistry is the branch of chemistry that studies organic compounds.

Carbon chains

All organic compounds contain the **element** carbon. Carbon **atoms** have a special **property** – each one can join with up to four other atoms. This means that carbon atoms can build up into very complex **molecules** with long chains containing thousands of carbon atoms, chains with branches off of them, and even rings. The two other main elements in organic compounds are oxygen and hydrogen.

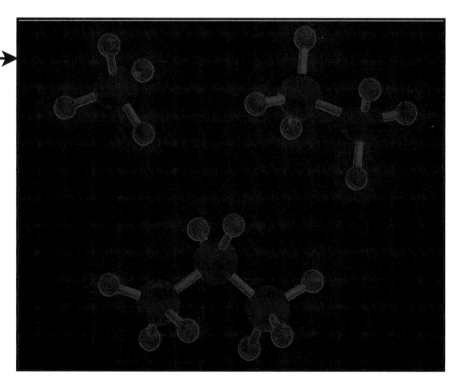

Models of molecules of the simple organic compounds methane (CH_4), ethane (C_2H_6) and propane (C_3H_8).

Compounds in living things

Animals and plants contain thousands of different organic compounds. Sugars, proteins and fats are examples of these organic compounds. One of the simplest organic compounds in our bodies is a sugar called glucose. Its formula is $C_6H_{12}O_6$.

Glucose is made in plants during a process called **photosynthesis**. It is broken down in animals and plants during a process called **respiration**. During respiration, energy is released. Here is the equation for the reaction that happens during respiration:

$$\text{glucose} \quad + \quad \text{oxygen} \quad \longrightarrow \quad \text{carbon dioxide} + \text{water}$$
$$C_6H_{12}O_6 \quad + \quad 6O_2 \quad \longrightarrow \quad 6CO_2 \quad \quad + 6H_2O$$

The energy released is used in animals and plants for growth and movement, and to make other **chemical reactions** happen. Sugars such as glucose are examples of compounds called carbohydrates because they contain only carbon, hydrogen and oxygen.

Proteins are very complex organic compounds. A protein molecule can contain many thousands of atoms. Proteins are the basic building blocks of **cells** and take part in many of the chemical reactions that make our bodies work. Fats are organic compounds that are stores of food for animals and plants. They are broken down into simpler substances that are used in respiration when the body needs some energy.

Materials from oil

The fossil fuel petroleum is a **mixture** of many organic compounds. Some of these compounds are quite simple, such as ethane (C_2H_6). Others are very complicated, and have molecules containing chains of 40 or more carbon atoms. Petroleum is separated into its parts by **fractional distillation** (see page 21). Some petroleum products, such as kerosene and butane, are used as fuels. Others are used as lubricants for machinery. Others are the raw materials that are used to make plastics.

This radio casing is made from bakelite, one of the first plastics, because it does not conduct electricity.

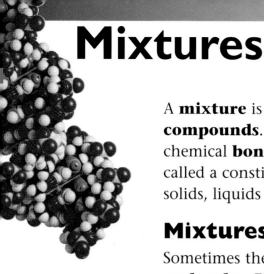

Mixtures

A **mixture** is a substance made up of different **elements** and **compounds**. The elements and compounds are not joined with chemical **bonds**. Each element or compound in a mixture is called a constituent. A mixture can have constituents which are solids, liquids or gases, or even all three together.

Mixtures of particles

Sometimes the **particles** in a mixture are individual **atoms** or **molecules**. For example, the air in the atmosphere is a mixture of molecules of different gases, such as nitrogen and oxygen. Sometimes the particles are clumps of atoms or molecules. For example, in a mixture of salt and granulated sugar, the particles are small crystals of salt and sugar. Each crystal contains millions of atoms. Sometimes a mixture contains individual atoms or molecules mixed with clumps of atoms or molecules. For example, smoke from a bonfire is a mixture of gas molecules and tiny specks of carbon, and muddy water is a mixture of water molecules and small pieces of rock.

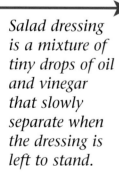

Salad dressing is a mixture of tiny drops of oil and vinegar that slowly separate when the dressing is left to stand.

Pure gold is described as 24-carat gold. Gold used in jewellery is mixed with other metals to make it harder.

Solutions

A **solution** is also a mixture. A solution is formed when a solid, a liquid or a gas dissolves in a liquid. For example, if you stir sugar into hot water, the sugar dissolves. It breaks up into individual sugar molecules. You end up with a solution that is a mixture of water molecules and sugar molecules. In a solution, the substance that dissolves (such as the sugar) is called the **solute** and the liquid it dissolves in (such as water) is called the **solvent**.

Pure substances

In chemistry, a pure substance is one that contains only one element or compound. Many substances that seem to be pure are not really pure because they contain small amounts of other materials. They are actually mixtures and the other materials in them are called impurities. For example, the water that comes out of your tap is not pure water. There are impurities such as calcium hydrogen carbonate dissolved in it. When the water is boiled, this forms calcium carbonate, which is left as scale in the kettle.

Separating mixtures

Because the parts of a mixture are not joined to each other with chemical bonds, a mixture can be separated into its constituents by physical processes. There are four main ways of separating mixtures and they are filtration, evaporation, distillation and chromatography.
You can find out how each of these work on the next four pages.

Separating mixtures

Chemists often need to separate **mixtures** into their different constituents. For example, they might need to **extract** a useful chemical from a mixture of chemicals, or they might want to purify a substance by removing the impurities from it. Alternatively, they might want to find out what substances are in a mixture.

Filtering

Filtering is used to separate a mixture of a liquid and an undissolved solid. The mixture is poured through filter paper, which has microscopic holes in it. The liquid can get through the holes but the solids cannot. For example, if you filter muddy water, the water **molecules** pass through the holes in the paper and can be collected in a beaker, but the particles of soil are trapped.

Chromatography

Chromatography is used to find out what the constituents of a mixture are. Scientists use chromatography to test whether substances are pure or to find whether two mixtures contain the same constituents. The simplest type of chromatography is paper chromatography. A blob of a mixture, such as ink (which is a mixture of dyes), is put on a piece of filter paper. The end of the paper is then placed in a **solvent** such as water. The solvent moves through the paper, carrying the dyes with it. Different dyes are carried different distances before they are left on the paper.

*A centrifuge is used to separate mixtures very quickly. As it spins at very high speed the most **dense** part of the mixture moves to the bottom of each tube.*

Experiment: Paper chromatography

PROBLEM: How can we find out whether the ink two pens use is the same?

HYPOTHESIS: We can use paper chromatography to find out what dyes are in the inks. If the dyes match, the inks are probably the same.

Experiment steps

EQUIPMENT
large jar
blotting (filter) paper
paper clip
selection of pens (not
    waterproof-ink pens)

1 Cut a piece of blotting paper about 10cm square. Choose two pens with the same colour of ink and put a spot from each pen about 2cm from the edge of the paper.

2 Pour 1cm of water into the jar. Fold the paper into a cylinder with the spots of ink at one end. Make it smaller than the jar so that it does not touch the sides. Stand it in the water with the spots at the bottom.

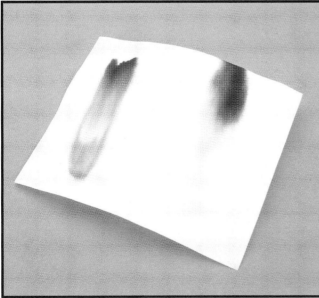

3 Observe what happens. When the water has reached the top of the paper, remove the paper and allow it to dry. Now compare the two sets of separated dyes.

CONCLUSION: If the patterns of dyes on the paper for each ink match, it is probable that the two inks are from the same manufacturer.

Evaporation

Evaporation is a method of getting a dissolved solid from a **solution**. You would use evaporation to **extract** the salt from salty water. The solution is put in a wide container so that a large area of solution is in contact with the air. The **solvent** gradually evaporates (in the same way a puddle dries up) and is lost into the air. The **particles** of the solid (or **solute**) do not evaporate. Eventually only the solid is left in the container.

Fractional distillation columns separate crude oil into petrol, natural gas and other useful products.

Distillation

Distillation is a method of getting a solvent from a solution. You would use distillation if you wanted to extract the water from salty water. The solution is put in a closed flask and heated until the solvent boils to make gas. The gas flows along a tube into a separate container where it cools and **condenses** back into liquid. The solute is left in the flask.

Fractional distillation

Fractional distillation is used to separate a **mixture** of liquids which have different **boiling points**. The mixture is put in a closed flask, and is gradually heated. Each liquid in the mixture boils at a different temperature to make a gas. The gases are collected and condensed to turn them back into liquids.

Experiment: Distillation

PROBLEM: How can we purify salty water?

HYPOTHESIS: By distilling the salty water. The liquid produced should be pure water. The salt will be left behind.

> **EQUIPMENT**
> large pan
> kitchen foil
> small bowl or dish
> ice
> salt

Experiment steps

1 Pour 1cm of water into a pan. Stir in two tablespoons of salt until the salt dissolves. Taste the water to see how salty it is. Ask an adult to help for the rest of the experiment.

2 Stand a small bowl in the centre of the pan. Cover the pan with kitchen foil. Gently press down the centre of the foil and put some ice cubes in the dip. Make sure that the dip in the foil stays above the small bowl, but is not tightly pressed into the small bowl itself.

3 Put the pan on the stove and heat it gently. After a few minutes remove it from the heat and allow it to cool. Make sure the pan does not boil dry.

4 When the pan is cool, taste the water in the small bowl. It should be pure, unsalted water. It has evaporated from the salty water, condensed on the foil and dripped into the small bowl. The ice keeps the foil cold so that condensation happens quickly underneath the foil.

CONCLUSION: Pure water (the solvent) has been successfully separated from the salt solution by distillation.

The periodic table

The periodic table is a chart of all the known **elements**. The elements are arranged in order of their atomic numbers, but in rows, so that elements with similar **properties** are underneath each other. The periodic table gets its name from the fact that the properties the elements have repeat themselves every few elements, or periodically. The position of an element in the periodic table gives an idea of what its properties are likely to be.

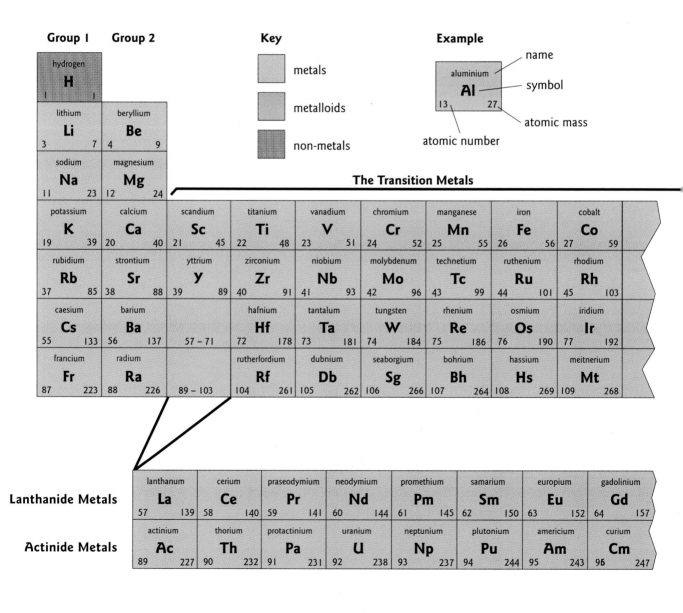

Key
- metals
- metalloids
- non-metals

Example

aluminium — name
Al — symbol
13 — atomic number
27 — atomic mass

Group 1	Group 2								
hydrogen **H** 1, 1									
lithium **Li** 3, 7	beryllium **Be** 4, 9								
sodium **Na** 11, 23	magnesium **Mg** 12, 24								

The Transition Metals

potassium **K** 19, 39	calcium **Ca** 20, 40	scandium **Sc** 21, 45	titanium **Ti** 22, 48	vanadium **V** 23, 51	chromium **Cr** 24, 52	manganese **Mn** 25, 55	iron **Fe** 26, 56	cobalt **Co** 27, 59
rubidium **Rb** 37, 85	strontium **Sr** 38, 88	yttrium **Y** 39, 89	zirconium **Zr** 40, 91	niobium **Nb** 41, 93	molybdenum **Mo** 42, 96	technetium **Tc** 43, 99	ruthenium **Ru** 44, 101	rhodium **Rh** 45, 103
caesium **Cs** 55, 133	barium **Ba** 56, 137	57 – 71	hafnium **Hf** 72, 178	tantalum **Ta** 73, 181	tungsten **W** 74, 184	rhenium **Re** 75, 186	osmium **Os** 76, 190	iridium **Ir** 77, 192
francium **Fr** 87, 223	radium **Ra** 88, 226	89 – 103	rutherfordium **Rf** 104, 261	dubnium **Db** 105, 262	seaborgium **Sg** 106, 266	bohrium **Bh** 107, 264	hassium **Hs** 108, 269	meitnerium **Mt** 109, 268

Lanthanide Metals

lanthanum **La** 57, 139	cerium **Ce** 58, 140	praseodymium **Pr** 59, 141	neodymium **Nd** 60, 144	promethium **Pm** 61, 145	samarium **Sm** 62, 150	europium **Eu** 63, 152	gadolinium **Gd** 64, 157

Actinide Metals

actinium **Ac** 89, 227	thorium **Th** 90, 232	protactinium **Pa** 91, 231	uranium **U** 92, 238	neptunium **Np** 93, 237	plutonium **Pu** 94, 244	americium **Am** 95, 243	curium **Cm** 96, 247

Groups and periods

The vertical columns of elements are called groups. The horizontal rows of elements are called periods. Some groups have special names:

Group 1: Alkali **metals**

Group 2: Alkaline earth metals

Group 7: Halogens

Group 0: Noble gases

The table is divided into two main sections, the metals and **non-metals**. Between the two are elements that have some properties of metals and some of non-metals. They are called semi-metals or **metalloids**.

Group 3	Group 4	Group 5	Group 6	Group 7	Group 0
					helium **He** 2 ... 4
boron **B** 5 ... 11	carbon **C** 6 ... 12	nitrogen **N** 7 ... 14	oxygen **O** 8 ... 16	fluorine **F** 9 ... 19	neon **Ne** 10 ... 20
aluminium **Al** 13 ... 27	silicon **Si** 14 ... 28	phosphorus **P** 15 ... 31	sulfur **S** 16 ... 32	chlorine **Cl** 17 ... 35	argon **Ar** 18 ... 40
gallium **Ga** 31 ... 70	germanium **Ge** 32 ... 73	arsenic **As** 33 ... 75	selenium **Se** 34 ... 79	bromine **Br** 35 ... 80	krypton **Kr** 36 ... 84
indium **In** 49 ... 115	tin **Sn** 50 ... 119	antimony **Sb** 51 ... 122	tellurium **Te** 52 ... 128	iodine **I** 53 ... 127	xenon **Xe** 54 ... 131
thallium **Tl** 81 ... 204	lead **Pb** 82 ... 207	bismuth **Bi** 83 ... 209	polonium **Po** 84 ... 209	astatine **At** 85 ... 210	radon **Rn** 86 ... 222
	ununquadium **Uuq** 114 ... 289				

Additional columns to the left (transition metals):

nickel **Ni** 28 ... 59	copper **Cu** 29 ... 64	zinc **Zn** 30 ... 65
palladium **Pd** 46 ... 106	silver **Ag** 47 ... 108	cadmium **Cd** 48 ... 112
platinum **Pt** 78 ... 195	gold **Au** 79 ... 197	mercury **Hg** 80 ... 201
ununnilium **Uun** 110 ... 271	unununium **Uuu** 111 ... 272	ununbium **Uub** 112 ... 285

terbium **Tb** 65 ... 159	dysprosium **Dy** 66 ... 163	holmium **Ho** 67 ... 165	erbium **Er** 68 ... 167	thulium **Tm** 69 ... 169	ytterbium **Yb** 70 ... 173	lutetium **Lu** 71 ... 175
berkelium **Bk** 97 ... 247	californium **Cf** 98 ... 251	einsteinium **Es** 99 ... 252	fermium **Fm** 100 ... 257	mendelevium **Md** 101 ... 258	nobelium **No** 102 ... 259	lawrencium **Lr** 103 ... 262

4 1

Common elements

Here is a table of the most common **elements** from the periodic table that you may come across at home or in the laboratory. The table indicates whether the element is a **metal** or **non-metal** and whether it is a solid, liquid or gas at room temperature.

Element	Symbol	Metal or not	State at room temperature
hydrogen	H	non-metal	gas
helium	He	non-metal	gas
lithium	Li	metal	solid
carbon	C	non-metal	solid
nitrogen	N	non-metal	gas
oxygen	O	non-metal	gas
fluorine	F	non-metal	gas
neon	Ne	non-metal	gas
sodium	Na	metal	solid
magnesium	Mg	metal	solid
aluminium	Al	metal	solid
silicon	Si	metalloid	solid
phosphorus	P	non-metal	solid
sulfur	S	non-metal	solid
chlorine	Cl	non-metal	gas
argon	Ar	non-metal	gas
potassium	K	metal	solid
calcium	Ca	metal	solid
iron	Fe	metal	solid
copper	Cu	metal	solid
zinc	Zn	metal	solid
bromine	Br	non-metal	liquid
silver	Ag	metal	solid
tin	Sn	metal	solid
iodine	I	non-metal	solid
gold	Au	metal	solid
mercury	Hg	metal	liquid
lead	Pb	metal	solid

Common chemicals

Here is a table of some common chemicals that you may come across at home or in the laboratory. The right hand column shows their formulae.

Gases

hydrogen ....H_2

oxygen ....O_2

chlorine...Cl_2

nitrogen ....N_2

carbon dioxide ....CO_2

nitrogen dioxide ....NO_2

Liquids and solutions

water...H_2O

hydrochloric acid..HCl

sulfuric acid...H_2SO_4

nitric acid ....HNO_3

sodium hydroxide...$NaOH$

Solids

sodium chloride ....$NaCl$

magnesium oxide..MgO

calcium carbonate...$CaCO_3$

copper sulfate...$CuSO_4$

Glossary of technical terms

acid liquid that can eat away metals and is neutralized by alkalis and bases. Acids have a pH below 7.

alkali liquid with a pH above 7

alloy material made by mixing a metal with another metal or a small amount of a non-metal. For example, steel is an alloy of iron and carbon.

atom extremely tiny particles of matter. An atom is the smallest particle of an element that can exist. All substances are made up of atoms.

base any chemical that neutralizes an acid. Some bases dissolve in water to make alkalis.

boiling point temperature at which a substance changes state from liquid to gas

bond join between two atoms, ions or molecules

cells tiny building blocks of plants and animals. All the parts of your body are made of different types of cells, such as nerve cells and blood cells.

chemical reaction happens when two chemicals (called the reactants) react together to form new chemicals (called the products)

compound substance that contains two or more different elements joined together by chemical bonds

condense to turn from a gas to a liquid. Gases normally condense when they cool.

conductor material that allows electricity (an electrical conductor) or heat (a heat conductor) to pass through it easily

decomposition type of chemical reaction in which a compound splits up into elements or more simple compounds

density amount of a substance (or mass) in a certain volume. Density is measured in grams per cubic centimetre or kilograms per cubic metre.

electrodes electrical contact that is touching a liquid in electrolysis

electrolysis method of separating a compound into its elements, using electricity

electron extremely tiny particle that is part of an atom. Electrons move around the nucleus of an atom.

element substance that contains just one type of atom. Elements are the simplest substances that exist.

extract remove from

formula collection of symbols and numbers that represents an element or compound. It shows what elements are in a compound and the ratio of the numbers of atoms of each element.

fractional distillation process of separating a mixture of liquids with different boiling points

insulator material that does not allow electricity (an electrical insulator) or heat (a heat insulator) to pass through it easily

ion type of particle. An ion is an atom that has lost or gained one or more electrons, giving it an overall positive or negative charge.

ionic compound compound made up of ions of different elements combined together

lattice structure made up of particles bonded together to form regular rows and columns

melting point temperature at which a substance changes state from solid to liquid as it warms

metal any element in the periodic table that is shiny, and that conducts electricity and heat well. Most metals are also hard.

metalloid element that cannot be classed as a metal or a non-metal. It has some of the properties of a metal and some of the properties of a non-metal.

micro-organism living thing too small to see without a microscope

mixture substance made up of two or more elements or compounds that are not joined together by chemical bonds

molecule type of particle. A molecule is made up of two or more atoms joined together by chemical bonds. The atoms can be of the same element or different elements.

natural gas gas often found deep underground with oil or coal, which is used as a fuel. It is made up mainly of the compound methane.

neutron one of the particles that makes up the nucleus of an atom

non-metal any element in the periodic table that is not a metal. Most non-metals are gases.

ore material dug from the ground that contains useful elements, such as iron, aluminium or sulfur

organic to do with living things. Organic compounds are compounds found in living things, or in the remains of living things.

oxide compound made when a metal or non-metal combines with oxygen

particle small piece of a substance. Particles can be atoms, ions, molecules or groups made up of atoms, ions or molecules joined together.

photosynthesis chemical reaction in which plants make food from water and carbon dioxide using the energy in sunlight

properties characteristics of a substance, such as its strength, melting point and density

proton one of the particles that makes up the nucleus of an atom

reactivity series list of common metals, arranged in order of how quickly they react with other substances, such as acids, water and air. The most reactive metals are at the top.

respiration chemical reaction in which animals and plants release energy from food

solution substance made when a solid, gas or liquid dissolves in a liquid.

solute substance that dissolves in a solvent to make a solution

solvent liquid that a substance dissolves in to make a solution

symbol single letter or two letters used to represent an element in chemical formulae and equations

unique only one

Further reading

Chemical Chaos (Horrible Science)
Nick Arnold, Tony de Saulles, Scholastic Hippo, 1997

Chemicals in Action
Ann Fullick, Heinemann Library, 1999

Co-ordinated Science, Chemistry Foundation
Andy Bethell, John Dexter, Mike Griffths, Heinemann, 2001

The Dorling Kindersley Science Encyclopedia
Dorling Kindersley, 1993

How Science Works
Judith Hann, Dorling Kindersley, 1991

The Usborne Illustrated Dictionary of Chemistry
Jane Wertheim, Chris Oxlade and Dr. John Waterhouse
Usborne, 1987

Useful websites

http://www.heinemannexplore.com
An exciting new online resource for school libraries and classrooms containing articles, investigations, biographies and activities related to all areas of the science curriculum.

http://www.creative-chemistry.org.uk
An interactive chemistry site including fun practical activities, worksheets, quizzes, puzzles and more! With links to many more useful and interesting sites including:

http://www.bbc.co.uk/science
Loads of information on all areas of science. Includes news, activities, games and quizzes.

http://www.chemicool.com
All you ever needed to know about the elements – and more!

http://www.webelements.com/webelements/scholar
The Periodic table – online! Discover more about all the elements and their properties.

http://particleadventure.org
An interactive site, explaining the fundamentals of matter and forces!

Disclaimer
All the Internet addresses (URLs) given in this book were valid at the time of going to press. However, due to the dynamic nature of the Internet, some addresses may have changed, or sites may have ceased to exist since publication. While the author and publishers regret any inconvenience this may cause readers, no responsibility for any such changes can be accepted by either the author or the publishers.

Index

Titles in the *Chemicals in Action* series include:

Hardback 0 431 13603 3

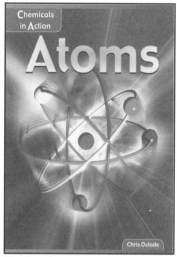

Hardback 0 431 13600 9

Hardback 0 431 13602 5

Hardback 0 431 13605 X

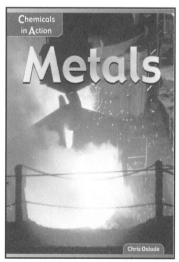

Hardback 0 431 13601 7

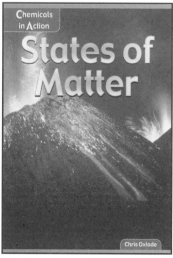

Hardback 0 431 13604 1

Find out about the other titles in this series on our website www.heinemann.co.uk/library